Pie Perfection Cookbook

© Copyright 2023. Laura Sommers.
All rights reserved.
No part of this book may be reproduced in any form or by any electronic or mechanical means without written permission of the author. All text, illustrations and design are the exclusive property of
Laura Sommers

Introduction 1

Pierogi Dough 2

Classic Pierogi with Potato and Cheese Filling 3

Sauerkraut Pierogi 4

Mushroom and Sauerkraut Pierogi 5

Mushroom and Spinach Pierogi 6

Blueberry Pierogi 7

Potato And Onion Pierogi 9

Potato And Cheddar Pierogi 11

Cottage Cheese Pierogi 13

Cheesy Bacon Pierogies 14

Loaded Baked Potato Pierogi 15

Nashville Hot Pierogi Bites 17

Herb Air-Fried Pierogies 18

Ranch Air Fried Pierogies 19

Pierogi Lasagna Bake 20

Pancetta Pierogies 21

BBQ Chicken Pierogi Nachos 22

Tomato Mushroom Pierogi Casserole 23

Cheesy Pierogi Quesadillas 25

Avocado Ranch Mini Pierogi Salad 26

Crunchy Pizza Pierogies 27

Perogies and Sausage Skillet 28

Reuben Pierogies 29

Bacon-Wrapped Pierogies 30

Pierogi Bruschetta 31

Pierogi Potato Salad 32

Sweet and Spicy Sriracha Mini Pierogies 33

Grilled Pierogi Kabobs 34

Buffalo Mini Pierogies 35

Caprese Pesto Pierogies 36

General Tso's Pierogies 37

Jalapeño Popper Pierogies 38

Maryland Style Pierogi Dippers 39

Philly Cheesesteak Pierogi Dumplings 40

Chicken & Waffles Pierogies 41

Kielbasa Pierogi Casserole 42

Spinach and Feta Pierogi 43

Jalapeño Cauliflower Pierogi Bake 44

Butternut Squash Pierogi Casserole 46

Chicken, Bacon, Ranch Pierogi Bake 48

Honey and Garlic Glazed Pierogies 49

White Pizza Pierogi Skillet 50

Shepherd's Pie Pierogies 51

Pierogies Alfredo 53

Pierogi Ramen 54

Pierogies Florentine 55

Teriyaki Pierogies 56

Spicy Pierogi Chili 57

Pierogies with Meatballs and Vodka Sauce 58

Swedish Meatballs and Pierogies 60

Tequila Lime Shrimp and Pierogies 62

Pierogi Mac and Cheese Skillet 63

Pierogi Taco Casserole 64

Tuscan Chicken Pierogi Skillet 65

Spanish-Style Pork and Pierogi Stew 67

Szechuan-Style Pierogies 68

Pierogi Scampi 69

Spanish-Style Pork and Pierogi Stew 70

Pierogi Pot Pie 72

Beer Battered Pierogies 73

About the Author 74

Other Books by Laura Sommers 75

Introduction

Welcome to the world of pierogies, a beloved dish that originated in Eastern Europe and has captured the hearts and taste buds of people all over the world. Pierogies are a comfort food that can be filled with an array of ingredients, from savory potatoes and cheese to sweet fruit and chocolate. They can be boiled, fried, baked, grilled, or sautéed, making them a versatile dish for any occasion.

In this cookbook, we'll take you on a culinary journey through the world of pierogies. You'll learn how to make traditional pierogies with classic fillings, as well as modern twists on the dish that will surprise and delight you. From savory pierogies with bacon and onions to sweet pierogies with blueberries and cream cheese, we've got something for every taste.

But that's not all – we'll also show you how to incorporate pierogies into other dishes, like casseroles, salads, and even desserts. You'll discover how versatile pierogies can be and how they can add a unique flavor and texture to any recipe.

Whether you're a pierogi aficionado or a newcomer to the dish, this cookbook has something for everyone. So grab your rolling pin and let's get cooking!

Pierogi Dough

Ingredients:

2 cups all-purpose flour
1/2 tsp. salt
1 large egg
1/2 cup sour cream
1/4 cup unsalted butter, softened
1/4 cup warm water

Directions:

1. In a large mixing bowl, combine the flour and salt.
2. In a separate bowl, whisk together the egg, sour cream, and butter until smooth.
3. Pour the egg mixture into the flour mixture and stir until well combined.
4. Gradually add the warm water to the mixture and knead the dough until it becomes smooth and elastic.
5. Cover the dough and let it rest for at least 30 minutes.
6. Roll out the dough on a lightly floured surface to about 1/8 inch thickness.
7. Use a biscuit cutter or glass to cut circles of dough.
8. Place a spoonful of your desired pierogi filling onto each circle of dough.
9. Fold the dough over to enclose the filling and seal the edges with a fork.
10. Place the pierogi onto a lightly floured surface and cover with a damp towel until ready to cook.
11. You can then boil the pierogi until they float to the surface of the water and are cooked through, then serve with your preferred toppings or sauce.

Classic Pierogi with Potato and Cheese Filling

Ingredients:

2 cups all-purpose flour
1 large egg
1/2 cup water
1/4 tsp salt
2 large potatoes, peeled and cubed
1/2 cup grated cheddar cheese
1/4 cup chopped onion
Salt and pepper, to taste
2 tbsp unsalted butter

Directions:

1. In a large mixing bowl, whisk together the flour and salt.
2. In a separate bowl, beat the egg and water together, and then add it to the flour mixture. Knead until a smooth dough forms.
3. Cover the dough with a damp towel and let it rest for 30 minutes.
4. While the dough is resting, boil the potatoes until tender.
5. Drain and mash them with the cheese, onion, salt, and pepper.
6. Roll the dough out on a floured surface and cut it into circles with a biscuit cutter.
7. Place a spoonful of the potato mixture in the center of each circle, then fold the dough over and pinch the edges to seal.
8. Boil the pierogi in salted water until they float to the surface, then remove and drain.
9. Heat the butter in a pan and fry the pierogi until golden brown on each side.
10. Serve hot.

Sauerkraut Pierogi

Ingredients:

2 cups all-purpose flour
1 large egg
1/2 cup water
1/4 tsp salt
1/2 cup sauerkraut, drained and chopped
1/4 cup finely chopped onion
1 tbsp olive oil
Salt and pepper, to taste

Directions:

1. In a large mixing bowl, whisk together the flour and salt.
2. In a separate bowl, beat the egg and water together, and then add it to the flour mixture. Knead until a smooth dough forms.
3. Cover the dough with a damp towel and let it rest for 30 minutes.
4. While the dough is resting, heat the olive oil in a pan and sauté the onion until soft.
5. Add the sauerkraut and cook for a few more minutes.
6. Roll the dough out on a floured surface and cut it into circles with a biscuit cutter.
7. Place a spoonful of the sauerkraut mixture in the center of each circle, then fold the dough over and pinch the edges to seal.
8. Boil the pierogi in salted water until they float to the surface, then remove and drain.
9. Serve hot.

Mushroom and Sauerkraut Pierogi

Ingredients:

2 cups all-purpose flour
1/2 tsp. salt
1 large egg
1/2 cup warm water
1 tbsp. vegetable oil
2 cups sauerkraut, drained and chopped
1 cup sliced mushrooms
1/2 cup chopped onion
1/4 cup butter
Salt and pepper to taste

Directions:

1. Follow steps 1-4 from the Classic Potato and Cheese Pierogi recipe above.
2. In a large skillet, melt the butter over medium heat.
3. Add the onion and sauté until softened and lightly browned.
4. Add the mushrooms and sauté for another 3-5 minutes, or until the mushrooms are tender.
5. Add the sauerkraut to the skillet and season with salt and pepper to taste.
6. Cook for another 2-3 minutes.
7. Fill each pierogi with a tbsp. of the mushroom and sauerkraut mixture, fold over, and pinch the edges to seal.
8. Bring a large pot of salted water to a boil.
9. Add the pierogi and cook for 2-3 minutes, or until they float to the surface.
10. Serve hot with a dollop of sour cream if desired.

Mushroom and Spinach Pierogi

Ingredients:

2 cups all-purpose flour
1 large egg
1/2 cup water
1/4 tsp salt
1 cup chopped mushrooms
1 cup chopped spinach
1/4 cup finely chopped onion
2 cloves garlic, minced
2 tbsp olive oil
Salt and pepper, to taste

Directions:

1. In a large mixing bowl, whisk together the flour and salt.
2. In a separate bowl, beat the egg and water together, and then add it to the flour mixture. Knead until a smooth dough forms.
3. Cover the dough with a damp towel and let it rest for 30 minutes.
4. While the dough is resting, heat the olive oil in a pan and sauté the onion until soft.
5. Add the mushrooms and garlic and cook for a few minutes, then add the spinach and cook until wilted.
6. Season with

Blueberry Pierogi

Ingredients:

2 cups all-purpose flour
1/2 tsp salt
1 large egg
1/4 cup sour cream
1/4 cup milk
1 1/2 cups fresh blueberries
2 tbsp granulated sugar
1/2 tsp ground cinnamon
1/4 tsp ground nutmeg
1/4 cup unsalted butter, melted
1/2 cup breadcrumbs
1/2 cup heavy cream

Directions:

1. In a large mixing bowl, whisk together the flour and salt.
2. In a separate bowl, whisk together the egg, sour cream, and milk.
3. Pour the wet ingredients into the dry ingredients, and mix until a dough forms.
4. Knead the dough on a floured surface for 10 minutes, until it becomes smooth.
5. Cover the dough and let it rest for 30 minutes.
6. While the dough is resting, mix together the blueberries, sugar, cinnamon, and nutmeg in a small bowl.
7. Roll out the dough on a floured surface, and use a round cookie cutter to cut out circles of dough.
8. Spoon a small amount of the blueberry mixture into the center of each dough circle.
9. Fold the dough in half, and use a fork to press the edges together and seal.
10. Bring a large pot of salted water to a boil.
11. Add the pierogi to the boiling water, and cook for 5-7 minutes, until they float to the surface.

12. Remove the pierogi from the water using a slotted spoon, and let them drain.
13. Melt the butter in a skillet, and add the breadcrumbs.
14. Cook the breadcrumbs until they are golden brown.
15. Serve the pierogi topped with the buttered breadcrumbs and a drizzle of heavy cream.

Potato And Onion Pierogi

Ingredients:

2 cups all-purpose flour
1/2 tsp. salt
1 large egg
1/2 cup lukewarm water
2 medium potatoes, peeled and diced
1 medium onion, diced
2 tbsps. butter
Salt and pepper to taste
1/4 cup sour cream

Directions:

1. In a mixing bowl, whisk together flour and salt.
2. Add the egg and lukewarm water, and mix until the dough comes together. Knead the dough for 5-7 minutes until it is smooth and elastic.
3. Cover the dough with a damp towel and let it rest for 30 minutes.
4. Meanwhile, boil the diced potatoes until they are soft.
5. Drain and mash them in a mixing bowl.
6. In a pan, melt the butter over medium heat and cook the diced onions until they are soft and golden brown.
7. Add the onions to the mashed potatoes and mix well.
8. Season with salt and pepper to taste.
9. On a floured surface, roll out the dough to 1/8 inch thickness.
10. Use a cookie cutter or a glass to cut out circles of dough about 3 inches in diameter.
11. Place a small spoonful of the potato and onion mixture in the center of each circle of dough.
12. Fold the dough over the filling and pinch the edges together to seal the pierogi.
13. Repeat until all the dough and filling are used up.
14. Bring a large pot of salted water to a boil.

15. Add the pierogi in batches and cook for about 5 minutes, or until they float to the top.
16. Remove the pierogi with a slotted spoon and transfer them to a serving dish.
17. Serve hot with a dollop of sour cream. Enjoy your delicious potato and onion pierogi!

Potato And Cheddar Pierogi

Ingredients:

2 cups all-purpose flour
1/2 tsp. salt
1 large egg
1/2 cup water
2 tbsps. vegetable oil
4 medium potatoes, peeled and cut into chunks
1 cup shredded cheddar cheese
1/2 tsp. salt
1/4 tsp. black pepper
1/2 cup butter
1 large onion, chopped

Directions:

1. In a large bowl, mix together the flour and 1/2 tsp. of salt.
2. Make a well in the center and add the egg, water, and vegetable oil.
3. Mix until the dough comes together, then knead on a floured surface for 5 minutes.
4. Cover and let rest for 30 minutes.
5. Meanwhile, cook the potatoes in boiling water until tender, about 15 minutes.
6. Drain and mash with a potato masher or fork.
7. Stir in the shredded cheddar cheese, 1/2 tsp. of salt, and black pepper.
8. On a floured surface, roll out the dough to about 1/8 inch thickness.
9. Cut circles using a biscuit cutter or glass.
10. Spoon about 1 tbsp. of the potato mixture onto each circle.
11. Fold the circle in half and pinch the edges together to seal.
12. Bring a large pot of salted water to a boil.

13. Add the pierogi and cook until they float to the top, about 3-4 minutes.
14. In a skillet, melt the butter over medium heat.
15. Add the chopped onion and cook until caramelized, about 10-15 minutes.
16. Serve the pierogi topped with the caramelized onions. Enjoy!

Cottage Cheese Pierogi

Ingredients:

2 cups all-purpose flour
1/2 tsp. salt
2 eggs
1/2 cup water
1 tbsp. olive oil
1/2 cup cottage cheese
1/4 cup grated Parmesan cheese
1/4 tsp. black pepper
1/4 tsp. salt

Directions:

1. In a large mixing bowl, combine flour and salt.
2. Make a well in the center of the mixture.
3. In a small bowl, whisk together eggs, water, and olive oil.
4. Pour into the well of the flour mixture and mix until a dough forms.
5. Turn the dough onto a floured surface and knead for 5 minutes until smooth.
6. Cover with a damp cloth and let rest for 30 minutes.
7. In a separate bowl, mix together cottage cheese, Parmesan cheese, black pepper, and salt.
8. Roll out the dough to 1/8 inch thickness and cut into 3-inch circles.
9. Place a tbsp. of filling in the center of each circle and fold in half, pinching the edges to seal.
10. Bring a large pot of salted water to a boil.
11. Add the pierogi to the pot and cook for 3-5 minutes until they float to the surface.
12. Drain the pierogi and serve with melted butter or sour cream. Enjoy!

Cheesy Bacon Pierogies

Ingredients:

1 lb. potato and cheese pierogies
4 slices bacon, chopped
1/2 onion, chopped
1/2 cup shredded cheddar cheese
2 tbsp. butter
Salt and pepper to taste
1/4 cup sour cream (optional)

Directions:

1. Cook pierogies according to package directions.
2. Drain and set aside.
3. In a large skillet, cook bacon over medium heat until crispy.
4. Remove from skillet and set aside.
5. Add onion to the same skillet and cook until softened.
6. Add butter and cooked pierogies to the skillet.
7. Cook until pierogies are lightly browned on both sides.
8. Add cooked bacon and shredded cheese to the skillet.
9. Stir until cheese is melted.
10. Season with salt and pepper to taste.
11. Serve hot with a dollop of sour cream, if desired.

Loaded Baked Potato Pierogi

Ingredients:

2 cups all-purpose flour
1/2 tsp salt
1 large egg
1/2 cup sour cream
1/4 cup unsalted butter, softened
1 lb russet potatoes, peeled and cubed
4 slices bacon, chopped
1/2 cup shredded cheddar cheese
1/4 cup chopped green onions
Salt and pepper, to taste
Sour cream and additional green onions, for serving

Directions:

1. In a large mixing bowl, combine the flour and salt.
2. Make a well in the center and add the egg, sour cream, and butter.
3. Mix well until a dough forms.
4. Turn the dough out onto a floured surface and knead for about 5 minutes until it becomes smooth and elastic.
5. Cover with plastic wrap and let rest for 30 minutes.
6. Meanwhile, boil the potatoes in salted water until tender.
7. Drain and mash with a potato masher or fork until smooth.
8. Set aside.
9. In a skillet, cook the bacon over medium heat until crisp.
10. Remove with a slotted spoon and drain on paper towels.
11. In a bowl, combine the mashed potatoes, bacon, cheddar cheese, and green onions.
12. Season with salt and pepper to taste.
13. Roll out the dough to about 1/8 inch thickness.
14. Use a round cutter or glass to cut out circles of dough.
15. Place a spoonful of the potato filling in the center of each dough circle.

16. Fold the dough over to form a half-moon shape and pinch the edges to seal.
17. Bring a large pot of salted water to a boil.
18. Add the pierogi and cook for 3-5 minutes until they float to the surface.
19. Remove with a slotted spoon and drain.
20. Serve the pierogi hot with a dollop of sour cream and additional chopped green onions. Enjoy!

Nashville Hot Pierogi Bites

Ingredients:

1 package of mini pierogies
1/2 cup all-purpose flour
1 tsp. smoked paprika
1 tsp. garlic powder
1 tsp. onion powder
1 tsp. cayenne pepper
1/2 tsp. salt
1/2 tsp. black pepper
1/2 cup buttermilk
1/4 cup hot sauce
1/4 cup unsalted butter, melted
2 tbsps. honey

Directions:

1. Preheat the oven to 400 degrees F.
2. Cook the mini pierogies according to the package directions.
3. In a shallow bowl, whisk together the flour, smoked paprika, garlic powder, onion powder, cayenne pepper, salt, and black pepper.
4. In another shallow bowl, whisk together the buttermilk and hot sauce.
5. Dip each cooked pierogi into the buttermilk mixture and then coat in the flour mixture.
6. Place the pierogi bites on a baking sheet and bake for 10-12 minutes, or until crispy.
7. In a small bowl, whisk together the melted butter and honey.
8. Once the pierogi bites are done, brush them with the honey butter mixture.
9. Serve immediately and enjoy the spicy and sweet flavor of Nashville hot pierogi bites!

Herb Air-Fried Pierogies

Ingredients:

1 box of Pierogies (16 pierogies)
1 tbsp olive oil
1 tsp dried basil
1 tsp dried oregano
1 tsp garlic powder
1/2 tsp salt
1/4 tsp black pepper
Marinara sauce, for dipping

Directions:

1. Preheat your air fryer to 400 degrees F.
2. In a small bowl, mix together the olive oil, dried basil, dried oregano, garlic powder, salt, and black pepper.
3. Brush the herb mixture onto both sides of each pierogi.
4. Place the pierogies in the air fryer basket in a single layer, making sure they don't touch.
5. Air fry for 8-10 minutes, flipping the pierogies halfway through, until they are golden brown and crispy.
6. Serve the pierogies hot with marinara sauce for dipping.

Ranch Air Fried Pierogies

Ingredients:

1 box of Pierogies
1/4 cup of ranch dressing
1/4 cup of bread crumbs
1/4 cup of grated Parmesan cheese
Salt and pepper to taste
Cooking spray

Directions:

1. Preheat air fryer to 400 degrees F.
2. Place pierogies in a single layer in the air fryer basket.
3. Spray the pierogies with cooking spray and cook for 8-10 minutes, flipping halfway through cooking.
4. While the pierogies are cooking, mix together the ranch dressing, bread crumbs, Parmesan cheese, salt, and pepper in a bowl.
5. Once the pierogies are finished cooking, transfer them to a bowl and toss with the ranch mixture until they are evenly coated.
6. Serve hot and enjoy!

Pierogi Lasagna Bake

Ingredients:

1 box of pierogi (16 oz)
1 lb ground beef
1 onion, chopped
2 cloves garlic, minced
1 jar of spaghetti sauce (24 oz)
1 cup of water
2 cups of shredded mozzarella cheese
Salt and pepper to taste
Cooking spray

Directions:

1. Preheat oven to 375 degrees F.
2. Cook pierogi according to package directions.
3. Drain and set aside.
4. In a large skillet over medium-high heat, brown ground beef until no longer pink.
5. Drain the fat.
6. Add onion and garlic to the skillet and sauté until tender.
7. Stir in spaghetti sauce and water.
8. Bring to a boil and reduce heat to low. Simmer for 5-10 minutes.
9. Spray a 9x13 inch baking dish with cooking spray.
10. Spread a thin layer of meat sauce in the bottom of the dish.
11. Arrange half of the pierogi in a single layer over the sauce.
12. Spread another layer of sauce over the pierogi and sprinkle with 1 cup of shredded mozzarella cheese.
13. Repeat with another layer of pierogi, sauce, and cheese.
14. Cover the dish with foil and bake for 25 minutes.
15. Remove the foil and bake for an additional 10-15 minutes, or until cheese is melted and bubbly.

16. Let the pierogi lasagna bake cool for a few minutes before serving.

Pancetta Pierogies

Ingredients:

1 package of pierogies
4 oz. pancetta, diced
1 small onion, diced
2 cloves garlic, minced
1/4 cup heavy cream
1/4 cup grated Parmesan cheese
Salt and pepper, to taste
Chopped parsley, for garnish

Directions:

1. Cook pierogies according to package directions.
2. While the pierogies are cooking, heat a large skillet over medium heat.
3. Add pancetta and cook until crispy, about 5-7 minutes.
4. Add onion to the skillet and sauté until softened, about 3-5 minutes.
5. Add garlic and cook for another minute.
6. Reduce heat to low and add heavy cream and Parmesan cheese to the skillet.
7. Stir until cheese is melted and mixture is heated through.
8. Season with salt and pepper, to taste.
9. Serve pierogies topped with the pancetta mixture and garnished with chopped parsley. Enjoy!

BBQ Chicken Pierogi Nachos

Ingredients:

1 box of pierogies
1 cup of cooked, shredded chicken
1/2 cup of your favorite BBQ sauce
1/4 cup of diced red onion
1/4 cup of chopped cilantro
1/4 cup of crumbled queso fresco
1 jalapeño, thinly sliced
1/4 cup of sour cream
Lime wedges

Directions:

1. Preheat oven to 425 degrees F.
2. Cook pierogies according to package instructions and set aside.
3. In a mixing bowl, combine the cooked, shredded chicken with the BBQ sauce until evenly coated.
4. On a baking sheet, spread out the cooked pierogies and top them with the BBQ chicken.
5. Sprinkle the red onion, cilantro, and queso fresco on top of the pierogies and chicken.
6. Place the baking sheet in the oven and bake for 10-15 minutes or until the pierogies are golden brown and the cheese is melted and bubbly.
7. Remove from the oven and top with jalapeño slices, a dollop of sour cream, and a squeeze of fresh lime juice.
8. Serve hot and enjoy!

Tomato Mushroom Pierogi Casserole

Ingredients:

1 package of pierogies (16 oz.)
1 lb. of ground beef
1 onion, chopped
1 can of diced tomatoes (14.5 oz.)
1 can of cream of mushroom soup (10.5 oz.)
1 cup of shredded cheddar cheese
Salt and pepper to taste
Optional: chopped fresh parsley for garnish

Directions:

1. Preheat the oven to 350 degrees F (175°C).
2. Cook the pierogies according to the package instructions and set them aside.
3. In a large skillet, cook the ground beef over medium heat until browned, breaking it up into small pieces as it cooks.
4. Add the chopped onion to the skillet and cook until softened.
5. Drain any excess fat from the skillet and add the diced tomatoes and cream of mushroom soup.
6. Stir until well combined.
7. Season the mixture with salt and pepper to taste.
8. In a greased 9x13 inch baking dish, layer half of the cooked pierogies on the bottom.
9. Pour half of the ground beef mixture over the pierogies.
10. Layer the remaining pierogies on top of the ground beef mixture, then pour the rest of the mixture over the pierogies.
11. Sprinkle the shredded cheddar cheese over the top of the casserole.
12. Cover the baking dish with foil and bake in the preheated oven for 25 minutes.

13. Remove the foil and bake for an additional 10-15 minutes, or until the cheese is melted and bubbly.
14. Garnish with chopped fresh parsley, if desired, and serve hot.

Cheesy Pierogi Quesadillas

Ingredients:

1 box of pierogies
4 large flour tortillas
1 cup shredded cheddar cheese
1/4 cup chopped green onions
1/4 cup sour cream
1/4 cup salsa
1 tbsp olive oil

Directions:

1. Cook the pierogies according to the package instructions, then set aside.
2. Heat the olive oil in a large non-stick skillet over medium-high heat.
3. Place one tortilla in the skillet and sprinkle 1/4 cup of the cheddar cheese on top.
4. Add 6 cooked pierogies on top of the cheese, then sprinkle another 1/4 cup of cheddar cheese on top of the pierogies.
5. Add 1 tbsp. of chopped green onions on top, then place another tortilla on top.
6. Cook the quesadilla for about 2-3 minutes on each side or until the cheese is melted and the tortillas are crispy.
7. Repeat the process for the remaining tortillas and pierogies.
8. Serve the quesadillas with a dollop of sour cream and a spoonful of salsa. Enjoy!

Avocado Ranch Mini Pierogi Salad

Ingredients:

1 package mini pierogies
1 avocado, diced
1/2 cup cherry tomatoes, halved
1/2 cup corn
1/4 cup red onion, diced
1/4 cup cilantro, chopped
1/4 cup ranch dressing
1 tbsp lime juice
Salt and pepper to taste

Directions:

1. Preheat the oven to 400 degrees F.
2. Cook the mini pierogies according to the package instructions.
3. While the pierogies are cooking, combine the diced avocado, cherry tomatoes, corn, red onion, and cilantro in a large mixing bowl.
4. In a small bowl, mix together the ranch dressing, lime juice, salt, and pepper.
5. Once the pierogies are cooked, drain them and add them to the mixing bowl with the other ingredients.
6. Pour the ranch dressing mixture over the pierogies and toss everything together until the pierogies are coated in the dressing.
7. Serve the salad chilled and enjoy!

Crunchy Pizza Pierogies

Ingredients:

1 box Pierogies
1/2 cup pizza sauce
1/2 cup shredded mozzarella cheese
1/4 cup grated Parmesan cheese
1/2 cup panko bread crumbs
1/4 tsp garlic powder
1/4 tsp onion powder
1/4 tsp dried oregano
1/4 tsp dried basil
Salt and pepper, to taste
2 tbsp olive oil

Directions:

1. Preheat oven to 400 degrees F.
2. Line a baking sheet with parchment paper.
3. Cook pierogies according to package instructions.
4. Drain and set aside.
5. In a small bowl, mix together panko bread crumbs, garlic powder, onion powder, dried oregano, dried basil, salt, and pepper.
6. Dip each pierogi in olive oil and then coat with the bread crumb mixture.
7. Place the coated pierogies on the prepared baking sheet and bake for 10 minutes.
8. Remove from oven and spread pizza sauce over each pierogi.
9. Top with shredded mozzarella and Parmesan cheese.
10. Return to oven and bake for an additional 5-7 minutes, until the cheese is melted and bubbly.
11. Serve hot and enjoy!

Perogies and Sausage Skillet

Ingredients:

1 pound of perogies
2 tbsps. of butter
1 onion, chopped
1 red bell pepper, chopped
1 green bell pepper, chopped
1 pound of smoked sausage, sliced
1 tsp. of paprika
1/2 tsp. of garlic powder
1/4 tsp. of salt
1/4 tsp. of black pepper
1 cup of shredded cheddar cheese

Directions:

1. Cook perogies according to package instructions, and drain.
2. In a large skillet, melt the butter over medium heat.
3. Add the onion and bell peppers, and sauté for 5 minutes, or until tender.
4. Add the sliced sausage to the skillet and continue to cook until lightly browned.
5. Stir in the paprika, garlic powder, salt, and black pepper.
6. Add the cooked perogies to the skillet and toss to combine with the sausage and vegetables.
7. Sprinkle the shredded cheddar cheese over the top of the perogies and sausage mixture.
8. Cover the skillet with a lid or aluminum foil and cook over low heat until the cheese is melted and bubbly, about 5 minutes.
9. Serve hot, garnished with chopped fresh parsley, if desired.

Reuben Pierogies

Ingredients:

1 box of pierogies
1/2 lb. corned beef, thinly sliced
1 cup sauerkraut, drained and rinsed
1 cup shredded Swiss cheese
1/4 cup Thousand Island dressing
2 tbsp. unsalted butter
Salt and pepper to taste

Directions:

1. Preheat the oven to 375 degrees F.
2. Cook pierogies according to the package instructions and drain well.
3. In a skillet over medium heat, melt the butter.
4. Add the cooked pierogies to the skillet and cook until lightly browned, about 2-3 minutes per side.
5. Remove the pierogies from the skillet and place them in a baking dish.
6. Top each pierogi with a slice of corned beef, a tbsp. of sauerkraut, and a sprinkle of Swiss cheese.
7. Bake the pierogies for 8-10 minutes, until the cheese is melted and bubbly.
8. Drizzle the Thousand Island dressing over the top of the pierogies before serving.
9. Season with salt and pepper to taste. Enjoy!

Bacon-Wrapped Pierogies

Ingredients:

1 package mini pierogies
1 lb. bacon
Toothpicks
Optional: dipping sauce of your choice

Directions:

1. Preheat oven to 400 degrees F (200°C).
2. Cut bacon strips in half and wrap each mini pierogi with a half slice of bacon. Secure bacon with a toothpick.
3. Place pierogies on a baking sheet lined with parchment paper.
4. Bake for 20-25 minutes, or until bacon is crispy and pierogies are heated through.
5. Remove toothpicks and serve with a dipping sauce of your choice, if desired. Enjoy!

Pierogi Bruschetta

Ingredients:

1 box of pierogies
1 tbsp. olive oil
1 tbsp. balsamic vinegar
1 garlic clove, minced
1/4 tsp. salt
1/4 tsp. black pepper
1/2 cup chopped tomatoes
1/4 cup chopped fresh basil
1/4 cup crumbled feta cheese

Directions:

1. Preheat the oven to 400 degrees F (200°C).
2. Cook the pierogies according to the package instructions, then drain and set aside.
3. In a small bowl, whisk together the olive oil, balsamic vinegar, minced garlic, salt, and black pepper.
4. Place the cooked pierogies on a baking sheet and brush them with the olive oil mixture.
5. Bake the pierogies in the oven for 10-12 minutes or until golden brown.
6. While the pierogies are baking, mix together the chopped tomatoes and chopped basil in a small bowl.
7. Top each pierogi with the tomato and basil mixture, then sprinkle with crumbled feta cheese.
8. Serve warm and enjoy!

Pierogi Potato Salad

Ingredients:

1 box (16 oz) Mini Pierogies
1 1/2 lbs baby potatoes
2 tbsp olive oil
1/2 cup diced red onion
1/2 cup diced celery
1/2 cup chopped fresh parsley
1/4 cup chopped fresh dill
1/2 cup mayonnaise
2 tbsp Dijon mustard
1 tbsp white wine vinegar
Salt and pepper to taste

Directions:

1. Cook the mini pierogies according to the package instructions.
2. Drain and set aside.
3. Cut the baby potatoes in half and place them in a large pot.
4. Cover with cold water and add a generous pinch of salt.
5. Bring to a boil and cook until the potatoes are tender, about 15 minutes.
6. Drain and let cool slightly.
7. In a large bowl, whisk together the mayonnaise, Dijon mustard, white wine vinegar, and salt and pepper.
8. Add the cooked mini pierogies, potatoes, red onion, celery, parsley, and dill to the bowl.
9. Gently toss until everything is well coated in the dressing.
10. Cover the bowl with plastic wrap and chill in the refrigerator for at least 30 minutes before serving.

Sweet and Spicy Sriracha Mini Pierogies

Ingredients:

1 package Mini Pierogies
2 tbsp unsalted butter
2 cloves garlic, minced
1/4 cup honey
1/4 cup Sriracha hot sauce
1 tbsp soy sauce
1 tbsp rice vinegar
1/2 tsp sesame oil
2 green onions, thinly sliced (optional)

Directions:

1. Cook the mini pierogies according to package instructions.
2. In a saucepan, melt the butter over medium heat.
3. Add the garlic and cook for 1-2 minutes until fragrant.
4. Add the honey, Sriracha, soy sauce, rice vinegar, and sesame oil to the saucepan.
5. Stir well to combine.
6. Cook the sauce for 2-3 minutes, stirring occasionally, until it thickens slightly.
7. Add the cooked mini pierogies to the saucepan and toss to coat with the sauce.
8. Serve hot, garnished with thinly sliced green onions if desired. Enjoy!
9. Note: Adjust the amount of Sriracha hot sauce to your desired level of spiciness.

Grilled Pierogi Kabobs

Ingredients:

1 package Mini Pierogies
1 red bell pepper
1 green bell pepper
1 yellow onion
1 zucchini
8-10 skewers
For the marinade:
1/4 cup olive oil
2 tbsps. balsamic vinegar
1 tbsp. Dijon mustard
1 tbsp. honey
2 cloves garlic, minced
Salt and pepper to taste

Directions:

1. Preheat your grill to medium-high heat.
2. Cut the bell peppers and onion into bite-sized pieces.
3. Cut the zucchini into thick slices.
4. In a small bowl, whisk together the olive oil, balsamic vinegar, Dijon mustard, honey, garlic, salt, and pepper.
5. Thread the pierogies, bell peppers, onion, and zucchini onto skewers, alternating ingredients.
6. Brush the kabobs with the marinade, making sure they are evenly coated.
7. Place the kabobs on the grill and cook for 8-10 minutes, turning occasionally, until the pierogies are golden brown and the vegetables are tender.
8. Serve immediately and enjoy!

Buffalo Mini Pierogies

Ingredients:

1 box Pierogies
2 tbsps. of unsalted butter
1/2 cup of hot sauce
1/4 tsp. of garlic powder
1/4 tsp. of paprika
1/4 tsp. of cayenne pepper
1/4 tsp. of salt
1/4 tsp. of black pepper
Ranch or blue cheese dressing, for serving

Directions:

1. Cook pierogies according to package directions.
2. Drain and set aside.
3. In a large skillet, melt butter over medium heat.
4. Add hot sauce, garlic powder, paprika, cayenne pepper, salt, and black pepper.
5. Whisk to combine.
6. Add cooked pierogies to the skillet and toss until coated in sauce.
7. Cook for an additional 2-3 minutes or until heated through.
8. Serve with ranch or blue cheese dressing for dipping. Enjoy!

Caprese Pesto Pierogies

Ingredients:

1 package pierogies
2 tbsp pesto sauce
1 large tomato, diced
8 oz fresh mozzarella cheese, diced
1 tbsp balsamic glaze
Salt and pepper, to taste
Fresh basil leaves, chopped

Directions:

1. Bring a large pot of salted water to a boil.
2. Add pierogies to the pot and cook for 5-7 minutes or until they rise to the top and are tender.
3. Drain the pierogies and set aside.
4. In a skillet over medium heat, add the pesto sauce and cook for 1-2 minutes until fragrant.
5. Add the diced tomato and cook for another 2-3 minutes until the tomato is soft and the flavors have melded together.
6. Add the cooked pierogies to the skillet and toss with the tomato and pesto mixture.
7. Add the diced mozzarella cheese and cook until melted and gooey.
8. Drizzle with balsamic glaze and season with salt and pepper to taste.
9. Top with chopped basil leaves and serve. Enjoy!

General Tso's Pierogies

Ingredients:

1 box (12.84 oz.) Pierogies
1/4 cup soy sauce
1/4 cup rice vinegar
3 tbsp. hoisin sauce
2 tbsp. honey
2 tbsp. ketchup
1 tbsp. chili paste
1 tbsp. minced garlic
1 tbsp. minced ginger
1 tsp. sesame oil
1 tsp. cornstarch
1 tbsp. vegetable oil
1/2 cup sliced scallions

Directions:

1. Cook Pierogies according to package directions.
2. In a medium bowl, whisk together soy sauce, rice vinegar, hoisin sauce, honey, ketchup, chili paste, garlic, ginger, sesame oil and cornstarch.
3. Heat a large skillet over medium-high heat.
4. Add vegetable oil and scallions, and cook for 2 minutes, stirring frequently.
5. Add cooked pierogies and sauce to skillet with scallions.
6. Cook for 2-3 minutes, stirring gently until pierogies are coated in sauce.
7. Serve pierogies with additional sliced scallions and sesame seeds, if desired.

Jalapeño Popper Pierogies

Ingredients:

1 package mini pierogies
6 slices of bacon
2 jalapeño peppers, seeded and diced
1/2 cup cream cheese, softened
1/2 cup shredded cheddar cheese
1/4 cup chopped green onions
Salt and pepper to taste

Directions:

1. Preheat oven to 375 degrees F.
2. Cook the pierogies according to package instructions, and set aside.
3. Cook bacon in a large skillet until crisp.
4. Remove from pan and drain on paper towels.
5. In the same skillet, cook diced jalapeño peppers until slightly softened, about 3-4 minutes.
6. In a mixing bowl, combine softened cream cheese, shredded cheddar cheese, and cooked jalapeños.
7. Season with salt and pepper to taste.
8. Cut cooked bacon into small pieces and mix into cheese mixture.
9. Arrange the cooked pierogies in a single layer in a greased 9x13 inch baking dish.
10. Spread the cheese mixture over the pierogies.
11. Bake for 20-25 minutes or until the cheese is melted and bubbly.
12. Garnish with chopped green onions before serving. Enjoy!

Maryland Style Pierogi Dippers

Ingredients:

1 package Mini Pierogies
8 oz lump crab meat
1/2 cup mayonnaise
1/4 cup finely diced red onion
1/4 cup finely diced celery
1 tbsp Old Bay seasoning
1 tsp lemon juice
1/4 tsp salt
1/4 tsp black pepper
1/4 cup panko breadcrumbs
2 tbsp unsalted butter, melted

Directions:

1. Preheat the oven to 400 degrees F.
2. Cook the mini pierogies according to package instructions.
3. In a mixing bowl, combine the crab meat, mayonnaise, red onion, celery, Old Bay seasoning, lemon juice, salt, and black pepper.
4. Mix well.
5. In another bowl, combine the panko breadcrumbs and melted butter.
6. Mix well.
7. Arrange the cooked pierogies on a baking sheet.
8. Spoon a small amount of the crab mixture onto each pierogi.
9. Sprinkle the breadcrumb mixture on top of the crab mixture.
10. Bake the pierogies for 10-12 minutes or until the topping is golden brown.
11. Serve hot and enjoy!

Philly Cheesesteak Pierogi Dumplings

Ingredients:

1 package pierogi (16-20 pierogi)
1 tbsp. vegetable oil
1/2 cup diced onion
1/2 cup diced green bell pepper
8 oz. thinly sliced beef (such as ribeye or sirloin)
Salt and pepper, to taste
1 cup shredded provolone cheese
1/2 cup beef broth
1 tbsp. Worcestershire sauce

Directions:

1. Cook pierogi according to package directions, then drain and set aside.
2. Heat oil in a large skillet over medium-high heat.
3. Add onions and peppers to the skillet and cook until softened, about 3-4 minutes.
4. Add sliced beef to the skillet and cook until browned, about 2-3 minutes.
5. Season with salt and pepper to taste.
6. Remove skillet from heat and add shredded provolone cheese to the skillet, stirring until cheese is melted and evenly distributed.
7. Spoon the beef and cheese mixture onto the cooked pierogi, then fold the pierogi over and press the edges together to seal.
8. In a small saucepan, combine beef broth and Worcestershire sauce and bring to a simmer.
9. Serve the pierogi dumplings with the beef broth sauce for dipping.

Chicken & Waffles Pierogies

Ingredients:

1 package Pierogies
2 cups fried chicken tenders, chopped
1/2 cup maple syrup
1/4 cup hot sauce
1/4 cup unsalted butter
1/4 cup all-purpose flour
2 cups whole milk
Salt and pepper, to taste
Waffle batter, prepared according to package instructions
Oil, for frying

Directions:

1. Cook pierogies according to package instructions.
2. Set aside.
3. In a small saucepan, combine maple syrup and hot sauce.
4. Heat over low heat until warmed through.
5. In a medium saucepan, melt butter over medium heat.
6. Whisk in flour until smooth.
7. Gradually whisk in milk.
8. Cook, whisking constantly, until mixture thickens and comes to a boil.
9. Season with salt and pepper to taste.
10. Reduce heat and keep warm.
11. Prepare waffle batter according to package instructions.
12. Preheat oil to 375 degrees F in a large pot or deep fryer.
13. Dip each pierogi in the waffle batter, shaking off excess batter.
14. Fry in the hot oil until golden brown and crispy, about 3-4 minutes.
15. Drain on a paper towel-lined plate.
16. To serve, place a few pierogies on a plate.
17. Top with chopped fried chicken tenders and drizzle with the maple hot sauce.

18. Serve with the warm white gravy on the side for dipping.

Kielbasa Pierogi Casserole

Ingredients:

1 package of frozen pierogies
1 pound of kielbasa, sliced
1 small onion, diced
1 tbsp. of vegetable oil
1 can of condensed cream of mushroom soup
1/2 cup of milk
1/2 cup of sour cream
1/4 tsp. of garlic powder
Salt and pepper to taste
1 cup of shredded cheddar cheese

Directions:

1. Preheat the oven to 375 degrees F.
2. Cook the pierogies according to package directions and set aside.
3. In a large skillet, heat the oil over medium heat.
4. Add the kielbasa and onion and cook until browned and caramelized, about 10 minutes.
5. In a bowl, whisk together the mushroom soup, milk, sour cream, garlic powder, salt, and pepper.
6. In a 9x13 inch baking dish, layer half of the pierogies on the bottom. Then, add a layer of the kielbasa mixture on top of the pierogies.
7. Pour half of the soup mixture over the kielbasa.
8. Repeat the layers, starting with the pierogies, followed by the kielbasa mixture, and then the remaining soup mixture.
9. Sprinkle the cheddar cheese on top of the casserole.
10. Cover the baking dish with foil and bake for 20 minutes.
11. Remove the foil and bake for an additional 10 minutes or until the cheese is melted and bubbly.
12. Let the casserole cool for a few minutes before serving.

Spinach and Feta Pierogi

Ingredients:

Pierogi dough
2 cups frozen chopped spinach, thawed and squeezed dry
1 cup crumbled feta cheese
1/4 cup grated Parmesan cheese
2 tbsps. chopped fresh parsley
1/4 tsp. garlic powder
Salt and pepper, to taste
1 egg, beaten
Butter or olive oil, for sautéing

Directions:

1. In a mixing bowl, combine the spinach, feta cheese, Parmesan cheese, parsley, garlic powder, salt, and pepper.
2. Roll out the pierogi dough to about 1/8-inch thickness, and cut out circles using a 3-inch biscuit cutter or a drinking glass.
3. Place a tbsp. of the spinach and feta mixture in the center of each circle.
4. Brush the edges of the circles with the beaten egg, and fold the dough over to create a half-moon shape.
5. Use a fork to crimp the edges shut.
6. Bring a large pot of salted water to a boil.
7. Add the pierogi to the pot and cook for about 3-4 minutes, or until they float to the surface.
8. Remove the pierogi with a slotted spoon and place on a plate.
9. Heat a skillet over medium-high heat and add a tbsp. of butter or olive oil.
10. Add the pierogi to the skillet and cook for 2-3 minutes per side, until they are golden brown and crispy.
11. Serve hot with sour cream or your favorite dipping sauce.

Jalapeño Cauliflower Pierogi Bake

Ingredients:

1 box Pierogies
4 cups cauliflower florets
1 tbsp olive oil
1/2 tsp salt
1/4 tsp black pepper
1/2 cup diced onion
2 jalapenos, diced
2 cloves garlic, minced
1 (14 oz) can diced tomatoes, drained
1/2 cup vegetable broth
1/2 tsp ground cumin
1/4 tsp chili powder
1/4 tsp paprika
1/2 cup shredded cheddar cheese
2 tbsp chopped fresh cilantro

Directions:

1. Preheat oven to 375 degrees F.
2. Cook pierogies according to package directions.
3. Drain and set aside.
4. In a large bowl, toss cauliflower florets with olive oil, salt, and black pepper.
5. Spread out in a single layer on a baking sheet and roast for 15 minutes, or until tender.
6. In a large skillet over medium-high heat, sauté onion and jalapenos until softened, about 5 minutes.
7. Add garlic and sauté for an additional minute.
8. Stir in diced tomatoes, vegetable broth, cumin, chili powder, and paprika.
9. Bring to a simmer and cook for 5 minutes.
10. Add pierogies and roasted cauliflower to the skillet and toss to coat with sauce.

11. Transfer the mixture to a 9x13 inch baking dish and sprinkle with shredded cheddar cheese.
12. Bake for 15-20 minutes, or until the cheese is melted and bubbly.
13. Sprinkle with chopped cilantro and serve hot.

Butternut Squash Pierogi Casserole

Ingredients:

2 cups all-purpose flour
1/2 tsp. salt
2 large eggs
1/3 cup water
1 tbsp. olive oil
1 small butternut squash, peeled, seeded, and diced
1/2 cup ricotta cheese
1/2 cup grated Parmesan cheese
1/4 tsp. nutmeg
Salt and pepper to taste
1/4 cup unsalted butter
1 small onion, finely chopped
1/2 cup chicken broth

Directions:

1. In a large mixing bowl, combine the flour and salt.
2. Make a well in the center and add the eggs, water, and olive oil.
3. Mix until a dough forms. Knead the dough on a floured surface for about 5 minutes, or until smooth.
4. In a separate pot, boil the butternut squash until tender.
5. Drain the squash and transfer it to a mixing bowl.
6. Mash the squash with a fork, then add the ricotta cheese, Parmesan cheese, nutmeg, salt, and pepper.
7. Mix well.
8. Roll out the dough on a floured surface until it is about 1/8 inch thick.
9. Cut the dough into circles using a biscuit cutter or glass.
10. Spoon a small amount of the butternut squash filling onto each circle of dough.
11. Fold the dough over to create a half-moon shape, and pinch the edges together to seal.

12. In a large pot of boiling salted water, cook the pierogies in small batches for about 3-4 minutes or until they float to the top.
13. Drain and set aside.
14. In a skillet, melt the butter over medium heat.
15. Add the onion and cook until softened, about 5 minutes.
16. Add the chicken broth and bring to a simmer.
17. Add the cooked pierogies to the skillet and toss with the onion and chicken broth mixture.
18. Serve hot. Enjoy!

Chicken, Bacon, Ranch Pierogi Bake

Ingredients:

1 package (16 oz) of pierogies
1 lb chicken breast, cubed
6 slices bacon, cooked and crumbled
1/2 cup ranch dressing
1/2 cup shredded cheddar cheese
1/4 cup chopped scallions

Directions:

1. Preheat the oven to 375 degrees F.
2. Cook the pierogies according to package instructions.
3. Drain and set aside.
4. In a large skillet over medium-high heat, cook the chicken until browned and cooked through.
5. In a large bowl, mix together the cooked pierogies, cooked chicken, bacon, ranch dressing, and half of the cheddar cheese.
6. Transfer the mixture to a 9x13 inch baking dish.
7. Sprinkle the remaining cheddar cheese over the top of the pierogi mixture.
8. Bake for 20-25 minutes or until the cheese is melted and bubbly.
9. Garnish with chopped scallions and serve hot.

Honey and Garlic Glazed Pierogies

Ingredients:

1 package of pierogies (16-20 pierogies)
3 tablespoons unsalted butter
3 garlic cloves, minced
2 tablespoons honey
1 tablespoon soy sauce
Salt and pepper to taste
Fresh parsley for garnish

Directions:

1. Cook pierogies according to package instructions. Drain and set aside.
2. In a pan over medium heat, melt butter. Add garlic and sauté until fragrant, about 1 minute.
3. Add honey and soy sauce to the pan and stir until the sauce is heated through.
4. Add the cooked pierogies to the pan and toss to coat with the sauce. Cook for an additional 2-3 minutes until pierogies are heated through and glazed with the sauce.
5. Season with salt and pepper to taste. Garnish with fresh parsley and serve hot.

White Pizza Pierogi Skillet

Ingredients:

1 package of pierogies (16-18 pieces)
1 tbsp. olive oil
2 garlic cloves, minced
1 cup ricotta cheese
1/2 cup grated Parmesan cheese
1/2 tsp. dried basil
1/2 tsp. dried oregano
Salt and pepper to taste
1 cup shredded mozzarella cheese
2 tbsps. chopped fresh parsley

Directions:

1. Preheat oven to 375 degrees F.
2. Cook pierogies according to package instructions.
3. In a skillet, heat olive oil over medium heat.
4. Add minced garlic and sauté for 1-2 minutes.
5. Add cooked pierogies to the skillet, and toss with the garlic.
6. In a mixing bowl, combine ricotta cheese, grated Parmesan cheese, dried basil, dried oregano, salt, and pepper.
7. Spread this mixture over the pierogies.
8. Top with shredded mozzarella cheese.
9. Bake in the preheated oven for 15-20 minutes, until the cheese is melted and bubbly.
10. Garnish with chopped parsley and serve hot.

Shepherd's Pie Pierogies

Ingredients:

1 package of pierogies
1 lb. of ground beef
1 onion, diced
2 cloves of garlic, minced
2 tbsp. of tomato paste
1 tbsp. of Worcestershire sauce
1 cup of beef broth
1 cup of frozen peas and carrots
1 cup of mashed potatoes
1/2 cup of shredded cheddar cheese
Salt and pepper to taste
Olive oil

Directions:

1. Preheat the oven to 375 degrees F.
2. Cook the pierogies according to the package directions and set aside.
3. In a large skillet, heat 1 tbsp. of olive oil over medium-high heat.
4. Add the ground beef and cook until browned, about 5 minutes.
5. Add the onion and garlic to the skillet and cook until the onion is translucent, about 3 minutes.
6. Add the tomato paste, Worcestershire sauce, and beef broth to the skillet.
7. Stir until everything is well combined.
8. Add the frozen peas and carrots to the skillet and stir to combine.
9. Cook for an additional 3-4 minutes, until the vegetables are tender.
10. In a separate bowl, mix together the mashed potatoes and cheddar cheese.

11. Spread the mashed potato mixture over the bottom of a 9x13-inch baking dish.
12. Arrange the cooked pierogies on top of the mashed potatoes.
13. Pour the beef mixture over the pierogies.
14. Bake the pierogies for 25-30 minutes or until the filling is heated through and the cheese is melted and bubbly.
15. Serve hot and enjoy!

Pierogies Alfredo

Ingredients:

1 package of pierogies (potato and cheese)
2 tbsp butter
2 cloves garlic, minced
1 cup heavy cream
1/2 cup grated Parmesan cheese
Salt and pepper, to taste
Fresh parsley, chopped (optional)

Directions:

1. Cook the pierogies according to the package instructions.
2. In a separate pan, melt the butter over medium heat.
3. Add the minced garlic and cook for 1-2 minutes until fragrant.
4. Add the heavy cream to the pan and bring to a simmer.
5. Reduce heat to low and add the grated Parmesan cheese, stirring constantly until the cheese has melted and the sauce has thickened.
6. Season with salt and pepper to taste.
7. Add the cooked pierogies to the sauce and toss to coat.
8. Serve with chopped fresh parsley on top, if desired.
9. Enjoy your delicious Pierogies Alfredo!

Pierogi Ramen

Ingredients:

4-5 pierogies
2 cups chicken or vegetable broth
1/2 cup sliced mushrooms
1/2 cup sliced onions
1/4 cup chopped scallions
1 tbsp minced garlic
1 tbsp soy sauce
1 tsp sesame oil
1 egg, soft-boiled
Salt and pepper to taste

Directions:

1. Cook pierogies according to package instructions, then set aside.
2. In a pot, sauté onions and garlic until fragrant, then add sliced mushrooms and continue cooking until they are soft.
3. Pour in chicken or vegetable broth and bring to a boil.
4. Add soy sauce, sesame oil, salt, and pepper, then reduce heat and let the broth simmer for a few minutes.
5. Place the pierogies in the broth and let them cook for another 2-3 minutes.
6. Serve the pierogies and broth in a bowl, then top with a soft-boiled egg and chopped scallions.

Pierogies Florentine

Ingredients:

1 package of pierogies
2 tbsps. of butter
1/2 small onion, chopped
2 cloves of garlic, minced
1/2 cup of chopped spinach
1/2 cup of heavy cream
1/4 cup of grated Parmesan cheese
Salt and pepper to taste

Directions:

1. Cook the pierogies according to the package instructions and set aside.
2. In a large skillet, melt the butter over medium heat.
3. Add the chopped onion and garlic to the skillet and cook until softened, about 3-4 minutes.
4. Add the chopped spinach to the skillet and cook until wilted, about 2-3 minutes.
5. Pour in the heavy cream and stir to combine.
6. Add the grated Parmesan cheese to the skillet and stir until melted and combined.
7. Season the sauce with salt and pepper to taste.
8. Add the cooked pierogies to the skillet and toss to coat them in the sauce.
9. Cook for an additional 1-2 minutes, until the pierogies are heated through and the sauce is thickened.
10. Serve immediately and enjoy!

Teriyaki Pierogies

Ingredients:

1 package of pierogies
1/4 cup soy sauce
1/4 cup mirin
1/4 cup honey
1/4 cup brown sugar
2 cloves garlic, minced
1 tsp grated ginger
1 tbsp cornstarch
2 tbsp water
2 tbsp vegetable oil
Sliced green onions, for garnish

Directions:

1. Cook the pierogies according to the package instructions and set aside.
2. In a small saucepan, whisk together the soy sauce, mirin, honey, brown sugar, garlic, and ginger.
3. Bring to a simmer over medium heat and cook for 2-3 minutes, stirring occasionally.
4. In a small bowl, whisk together the cornstarch and water until smooth.
5. Add the cornstarch mixture to the teriyaki sauce and whisk to combine. Simmer for an additional 1-2 minutes until the sauce thickens.
6. In a large skillet, heat the vegetable oil over medium-high heat.
7. Add the cooked pierogies and cook until they are lightly browned, about 2-3 minutes per side.
8. Pour the teriyaki sauce over the pierogies in the skillet and stir to coat.
9. Cook for an additional 1-2 minutes until the sauce is heated through and the pierogies are evenly coated.

10. Serve the teriyaki pierogies hot, garnished with sliced green onions.

Spicy Pierogi Chili

Ingredients:

1 package of pierogies (frozen or homemade)
1 pound of ground beef
1 onion, diced
2 cloves of garlic, minced
1 green bell pepper, diced
1 red bell pepper, diced
1 can of kidney beans, drained and rinsed
1 can of diced tomatoes
1 cup of tomato sauce
2 tbsps. of chili powder
1 tsp. of cumin
1 tsp. of paprika
1/2 tsp. of cayenne pepper
Salt and pepper, to taste
Shredded cheddar cheese and sour cream for garnish (optional)

Directions:

1. Cook pierogies according to package directions or prepare homemade pierogies.
2. In a large pot or Dutch oven, cook the ground beef over medium-high heat until browned.
3. Drain any excess fat.
4. Add the diced onion, garlic, and bell peppers to the pot and cook until vegetables are tender.
5. Add the kidney beans, diced tomatoes, tomato sauce, chili powder, cumin, paprika, and cayenne pepper to the pot.
6. Stir well to combine.
7. Add the cooked pierogies to the pot and stir gently to coat them in the sauce.
8. Bring the mixture to a simmer and let cook for 10-15 minutes, or until the sauce has thickened and the pierogies are heated through.

9. Serve hot, topped with shredded cheddar cheese and a dollop of sour cream, if desired. Enjoy!

Pierogies with Meatballs and Vodka Sauce

Ingredients:

1 package of pierogies
1 lb. ground beef
1/2 cup bread crumbs
1 egg
1/4 cup milk
1/2 cup grated parmesan cheese
1/4 cup chopped fresh parsley
1/4 tsp. salt
1/4 tsp. black pepper
2 tbsp. olive oil
1 onion, chopped
2 cloves garlic, minced
1 can crushed tomatoes (28 oz.)
1/4 cup vodka
1/2 cup heavy cream
Salt and pepper, to taste

Directions:

1. Preheat oven to 375 degrees F.
2. Cook the pierogies according to the package instructions.
3. In a large mixing bowl, combine the ground beef, bread crumbs, egg, milk, parmesan cheese, parsley, salt, and black pepper.
4. Mix well and form into meatballs.
5. In a large skillet, heat the olive oil over medium heat.
6. Add the meatballs and cook until browned on all sides.
7. Add the onion and garlic to the skillet and cook until softened.
8. Pour in the crushed tomatoes and vodka.
9. Bring to a simmer and cook for 10-15 minutes.
10. Add the heavy cream and stir until well combined. Simmer for an additional 5 minutes.

11. Season with salt and pepper to taste.
12. Add the cooked pierogies to the skillet with the meatball and vodka sauce mixture.
13. Gently stir until the pierogies are coated with the sauce.
14. Transfer the pierogies and sauce to a baking dish.
15. Bake in the preheated oven for 10-15 minutes, until heated through and slightly browned on top.
16. Serve hot and enjoy!

Swedish Meatballs and Pierogies

Ingredients:

1 package of pierogies
1 pound ground beef
1 egg
1/2 cup breadcrumbs
1/4 cup finely chopped onion
1/4 tsp. nutmeg
1/4 tsp. allspice
1/4 tsp. black pepper
1/4 cup butter
1/4 cup flour
2 cups beef broth
1 cup heavy cream
1/4 cup sour cream
1 tbsp. Worcestershire sauce
1 tbsp. Dijon mustard
1/4 cup chopped fresh parsley
Salt and pepper, to taste

Directions:

1. Preheat the oven to 350 degrees F.
2. Cook the pierogies according to the package directions and set aside.
3. In a large bowl, mix together the ground beef, egg, breadcrumbs, onion, nutmeg, allspice, black pepper, and a pinch of salt.
4. Roll the mixture into small meatballs.
5. In a large skillet, melt the butter over medium heat.
6. Add the meatballs and cook until browned on all sides and cooked through, about 10-12 minutes.
7. Remove the meatballs from the skillet and set aside.
8. In the same skillet, whisk in the flour and cook for 1-2 minutes until browned. Slowly whisk in the beef broth and heavy cream until smooth.

9. Bring the mixture to a simmer and cook until thickened, about 5-7 minutes.
10. Stir in the sour cream, Worcestershire sauce, Dijon mustard, parsley, and salt and pepper to taste.
11. Add the cooked pierogies and meatballs to the sauce and gently stir to combine.
12. Heat until warmed through.
13. Serve hot and enjoy!

Tequila Lime Shrimp and Pierogies

Ingredients:

1 lb shrimp, peeled and deveined
1/4 cup tequila
Juice of 2 limes
2 tbsp olive oil
1 tbsp honey
2 cloves garlic, minced
1 tsp chili powder
Salt and pepper, to taste
Corn or flour tortillas
Shredded cabbage or lettuce
Diced tomatoes
Shredded cheese
Cilantro, chopped
Sour cream

Directions:

1. In a bowl, whisk together the tequila, lime juice, olive oil, honey, garlic, chili powder, salt, and pepper.
2. Add the shrimp to the bowl and toss to coat.
3. Cover and refrigerate for at least 30 minutes.
4. Heat a large skillet over medium-high heat.
5. Add the shrimp and marinade and cook until the shrimp are pink and cooked through, about 3-4 minutes per side.
6. To assemble the tacos, warm the tortillas in a dry skillet or in the microwave.
7. Top each tortilla with some shredded cabbage or lettuce, diced tomatoes, and shrimp.
8. Sprinkle with shredded cheese and cilantro. Drizzle with sour cream, if desired.

Pierogi Mac and Cheese Skillet

Ingredients:

1 box (16 oz) pierogies
2 cups uncooked elbow macaroni
1/4 cup unsalted butter
1/4 cup all-purpose flour
3 cups whole milk
2 cups shredded cheddar cheese
1/2 cup sour cream
1 tsp dijon mustard
1 tsp garlic powder
1 tsp onion powder
Salt and pepper to taste

Directions:

1. Preheat the oven to 375 degrees F.
2. Cook pierogies according to package instructions.
3. Drain and set aside.
4. Cook elbow macaroni according to package instructions.
5. Drain and set aside.
6. In a large skillet, melt butter over medium heat.
7. Add flour and whisk until smooth.
8. Gradually add in the milk, whisking constantly, until the mixture thickens.
9. Add shredded cheddar cheese, sour cream, dijon mustard, garlic powder, onion powder, salt, and pepper.
10. Stir until the cheese is melted and the mixture is smooth.
11. Add the cooked pierogies and elbow macaroni to the skillet and stir until evenly coated with the cheese sauce.
12. Transfer the skillet to the preheated oven and bake for 15-20 minutes, until the top is golden brown and the cheese is bubbly.
13. Serve hot and enjoy!

Pierogi Taco Casserole

Ingredients:

1 package of pierogies
1 lb. ground beef
1 packet of taco seasoning
1 can of diced tomatoes
1 can of corn
1 small can of sliced black olives
1 cup of shredded cheddar cheese
1 cup of sour cream
Sliced green onions for garnish

Directions:

1. Preheat the oven to 375 degrees F.
2. Cook the pierogies according to the package directions and set them aside.
3. Brown the ground beef in a large skillet over medium-high heat.
4. Add the taco seasoning, diced tomatoes, and corn to the skillet and stir to combine.
5. Simmer for 5-10 minutes or until the mixture has thickened slightly.
6. Grease a 9x13 inch baking dish with cooking spray.
7. Layer the pierogies on the bottom of the baking dish.
8. Pour the beef mixture over the pierogies and spread it evenly.
9. Sprinkle the black olives and shredded cheddar cheese on top of the beef mixture.
10. Bake for 15-20 minutes or until the cheese is melted and bubbly.
11. Garnish with sliced green onions and serve with a dollop of sour cream on top. Enjoy!

Tuscan Chicken Pierogi Skillet

Ingredients:

1 package of pierogies (16-18 pierogies)
2 boneless, skinless chicken breasts, cut into cubes
1 tbsp. olive oil
4 cloves garlic, minced
1 tsp. dried oregano
1 tsp. dried basil
1/2 tsp. dried thyme
1/2 tsp. salt
1/4 tsp. black pepper
1/2 cup sun-dried tomatoes, chopped
1/2 cup chicken broth
1/2 cup heavy cream
1/4 cup grated Parmesan cheese
2 cups fresh spinach leaves
Fresh basil leaves, chopped, for garnish

Directions:

1. Cook the pierogies according to the package instructions.
2. Drain and set aside.
3. Heat the olive oil in a large skillet over medium-high heat.
4. Add the chicken and cook for 5-7 minutes, or until golden brown and cooked through.
5. Add the garlic, oregano, basil, thyme, salt, and pepper to the skillet.
6. Cook for 1-2 minutes, or until fragrant.
7. Add the sun-dried tomatoes and chicken broth to the skillet.
8. Bring to a simmer and let cook for 5 minutes, or until the sauce has reduced slightly.
9. Stir in the heavy cream and Parmesan cheese until well combined.
10. Add the spinach and cook for 1-2 minutes, or until wilted.

11. Add the cooked pierogies to the skillet and toss to coat with the sauce.
12. Garnish with fresh basil leaves and serve hot.

Spanish-Style Pork and Pierogi Stew

Ingredients:

1 lb. pork shoulder, trimmed and cut into bite-sized pieces
1 onion, chopped
2 garlic cloves, minced
2 bell peppers, chopped
1 can diced tomatoes, drained
2 cups chicken or vegetable broth
1 tsp. smoked paprika
1 tsp. dried oregano
1 tsp. ground cumin
1 bay leaf
Salt and pepper, to taste
1 package of pierogies, cooked according to package
Directions:
1. Chopped fresh parsley, for garnish
2. Directions:
3. In a large pot or Dutch oven, heat some oil over medium heat.
4. Add the pork and cook until browned on all sides.
5. Remove from the pot and set aside.
6. Add the onion, garlic, and bell peppers to the pot and sauté until softened.
7. Add the canned tomatoes, broth, paprika, oregano, cumin, bay leaf, salt, and pepper.
8. Stir to combine.
9. Add the pork back to the pot and bring the mixture to a boil.
10. Reduce the heat to low and simmer for about 45 minutes, or until the pork is tender and the stew has thickened.
11. Add the cooked pierogies to the stew and stir gently to combine.
12. Serve the stew hot, garnished with chopped parsley.

Szechuan-Style Pierogies

Ingredients:

1 package of pierogies
1 tbsp. vegetable oil
1/2 pound ground pork
1/2 tsp. salt
1/4 tsp. pepper
2 cloves garlic, minced
1 tsp. ginger, minced
2 tbsps. soy sauce
2 tbsps. Szechuan sauce
1/4 cup chicken broth
1/4 cup chopped green onions

Directions:

1. Cook the pierogies according to the package instructions and set aside.
2. Heat the vegetable oil in a large skillet over medium-high heat.
3. Add the ground pork, salt, and pepper, and cook until browned, about 5-7 minutes.
4. Add the minced garlic and ginger to the skillet and cook for 1-2 minutes, until fragrant.
5. Stir in the soy sauce, Szechuan sauce, and chicken broth, and bring to a simmer.
6. Add the cooked pierogies to the skillet and toss to coat in the sauce.
7. Cook for 2-3 minutes, until the pierogies are heated through and the sauce has thickened slightly.
8. Serve hot, garnished with chopped green onions.

Pierogi Scampi

Ingredients:

1 package (16 oz) pierogies
1/2 cup butter
4 cloves garlic, minced
1/2 cup white wine
1/4 cup lemon juice
1/4 cup chopped parsley
1/4 tsp red pepper flakes
1 lb large shrimp, peeled and deveined
Salt and pepper, to taste

Directions:

1. Cook pierogies according to package instructions.
2. Drain and set aside.
3. Melt butter in a large skillet over medium heat.
4. Add garlic and sauté until fragrant, about 1 minute.
5. Add white wine, lemon juice, chopped parsley, and red pepper flakes to the skillet.
6. Stir to combine.
7. Add the shrimp to the skillet and cook until pink and cooked through, about 3-4 minutes.
8. Season with salt and pepper, to taste.
9. Add the cooked pierogies to the skillet and toss to coat with the sauce.
10. Serve hot, garnished with additional chopped parsley if desired.

Spanish-Style Pork and Pierogi Stew

Ingredients:

1 lb. pork shoulder, cubed
2 tbsp. olive oil
1 onion, chopped
3 cloves garlic, minced
1 red bell pepper, chopped
1 green bell pepper, chopped
2 cups chicken broth
1 can diced tomatoes (14.5 oz)
1 tsp. smoked paprika
1/2 tsp. ground cumin
1/2 tsp. dried oregano
1/2 tsp. salt
1/4 tsp. black pepper
1 package of pierogies (16 oz)

Directions:

1. In a large pot or Dutch oven, heat olive oil over medium heat.
2. Add pork and cook until browned on all sides, about 5-7 minutes.
3. Add onion, garlic, red and green bell peppers and sauté for about 5 minutes or until vegetables are soft.
4. Stir in chicken broth, diced tomatoes, smoked paprika, ground cumin, dried oregano, salt, and black pepper.
5. Bring to a boil.
6. Reduce heat to low, cover and simmer for about 30 minutes or until pork is tender.
7. In the meantime, cook pierogies according to package directions.
8. Once the pork is tender, add the cooked pierogies to the stew and stir to combine.
9. Cook for an additional 5-10 minutes or until pierogies are heated through.

10. Serve hot, garnished with chopped parsley if desired. Enjoy!

Pierogi Pot Pie

Ingredients:

1 package of frozen pierogies (16-18 pierogies)
1 pound of chicken, cut into bite-sized pieces
1 cup of frozen mixed vegetables (peas, carrots, corn, green beans)
1 can of condensed cream of mushroom soup
1/2 cup of milk
1/2 cup of chicken broth
1/2 tsp. of garlic powder
Salt and pepper, to taste
1 pie crust

Directions:

1. Preheat your oven to 375 degrees F (190°C).
2. In a skillet, cook the chicken over medium-high heat until browned on all sides.
3. Add the mixed vegetables to the skillet and cook until they are heated through.
4. In a separate bowl, whisk together the cream of mushroom soup, milk, chicken broth, garlic powder, salt, and pepper.
5. Add the sauce to the skillet with the chicken and vegetables, and stir to combine.
6. Add the frozen pierogies to the skillet and stir to coat them with the sauce.
7. Roll out the pie crust and place it on top of the skillet, crimping the edges to seal it.
8. Cut a few small slits in the top of the crust to allow steam to escape.
9. Bake the pot pie for 30-35 minutes, until the crust is golden brown and the filling is bubbling.
10. Let the pot pie cool for a few minutes before serving.

Beer Battered Pierogies

Ingredients:

12 pierogies
1 cup all-purpose flour
1 tsp. baking powder
1/2 tsp. salt
1/4 tsp. black pepper
1 egg
1/2 cup beer (your choice of lager or pilsner)
1/4 cup milk
Oil for frying

Directions:

1. Preheat the oven to 200 degrees F to keep the pierogies warm after frying.
2. Cook the pierogies according to the package instructions, and then pat them dry with paper towels.
3. In a mixing bowl, combine the flour, baking powder, salt, and black pepper.
4. In a separate mixing bowl, whisk the egg, beer, and milk together.
5. Gradually add the dry ingredients into the wet mixture, whisking until the batter is smooth.
6. In a heavy-bottomed pan, heat enough oil over medium-high heat to fry the pierogies.
7. Dip each pierogi into the batter, coating it evenly.
8. Carefully place each coated pierogi into the hot oil, and fry until golden brown and crispy.
9. Use a slotted spoon to remove the pierogies from the oil, and place them on a paper towel to drain the excess oil.
10. Once all pierogies are fried, place them in the preheated oven to keep warm until ready to serve.
11. Enjoy your beer-battered pierogies with your favorite dipping sauce, such as sour cream or a spicy aioli.

About the Author

Laura Sommers is **The Recipe Lady!**

She lives on a small farm in Baltimore County, Maryland and has a passion for food. She has taken cooking classes in New York City, Memphis, New Orleans and Washington DC. She has been a taste tester for a large spice company in Baltimore and written food reviews for several local papers. She loves writing cookbooks with the most delicious recipes to share her knowledge and love of cooking with the world.

Follow her on Pinterest:

http://pinterest.com/therecipelady1

Visit the Recipe Lady's blog for even more great recipes:

http://the-recipe-lady.blogspot.com/

Visit her Amazon Author Page to see her latest books:

amazon.com/author/laurasommers

Follow the Recipe Lady on Facebook:

https://www.facebook.com/therecipegirl

Follow her on Twitter:

https://twitter.com/TheRecipeLady1

Other Books by Laura Sommers

Irish Recipes for St. Patrick's Day

Traditional Vermont Recipes

Traditional Memphis Recipes

Maryland Chesapeake Bay Blue Crab Cookbook

Mussels Cookbook

Maryland Chesapeake Bay Blue Crab Cookbook

Salmon Recipes

Scallop Recipes

A Taste of Pittsburgh Cookbook

Made in the USA
Monee, IL
05 October 2023